How to
Motivate
Manage
& Market
Yourself

To Kip &

You are ...... winners!

Thanks!

Love

Lisa

How to

Motivate

Manage

& Market

Yourself

Lisa McInnes-Smith • Daniel Johnson • Winston Marsh

Published as a joint venture by:
Winston Marsh Pty. Ltd.
10 Johnson St
Oakleigh 3166
Webster Human Resources Pty. Ltd.
trading as
Daniel Johnson Presentations
254 North Rd
Brighton East 3187
Cassette Learning Systems Pty. Ltd.
7 Panorama Crt
Bulleen
Victoria 3105

First published in this edition 1989

Reprinted 1989

Reprinted 1990

Reprinted 1991 (twice)

Reprinted 1992 (twice)

Reprinted 1994

Printed by McPherson's Printing Group, Mulgrave, Vic.

Typeset by Bookset, North Melbourne, Vic.

ISBN 0 958 8604 6 7

This book is dedicated to You, the reader. Our aim is to help you to live a happier and more productive life. Just as others have shared their knowledge with us, so we share our knowledge with you. We hope that you will act upon it and enjoy its fruits.

CONTENTS

PART 1

How to Motivate Yourself

PART 2

How to Manage Yourself

PART 3

How to Market Yourself

Lisa McInnes-Smith is the esteemed author of two best selling books, 'Why Wasn't I Told' and 'I'm A Walking, Talking Miracle', on motivation and achievement. Lisa is acclaimed throughout Australia for her unique ability to inspire and teach people how to motivate themselves and others. She is one of Australia's most sought after speakers. Lisa's Christian commitment has enabled her to positively affect the lives of over one million young Australians.

PART 1

HOW TO
Motivate
YOURSELF

by
Lisa McInnes-Smith

What's your motive?

He who learns to laugh at himself will never cease to be entertained.

O ne of the greatest untruths about motivation is this: Motivation doesn't last so it's not worth the effort, time or money.

However, the truth is this:

Motivation doesn't last so we need a dose every day.

While studying successful people it has become evident to me that those who achieve their personal worthwhile goals (otherwise known as success), give themselves some daily motivation.

So what is this thing called motivation? Described in very simple terms, it is a motive for action or a reason for doing. I would go as far as saying it is the result of knowing your purpose for living.

Without motivation, nothing gets done. Does that sound familiar?

So ask yourself: What is my motive for taking action today? There is a big difference between getting out of bed just to earn the money to pay the bills and getting out of bed to discover a cure for cancer or create a way to feed the poor. Some people are so excited in the morning they can't wait to get going. Others can't wait for the day to be over so they can return to bed. How do you want to wake up? Is there something you would really like to do with your life?

If you know what you want and why, you can work out how.

Although my goals have changed often during the last ten years, I have continually attempted to focus on one major project at a time. At the moment my desire is to positively affect and influence the lives of one million Australian youth. That gets me excited. And it gets me going in the morning. So what about you? Do you have a goal that excites you?

The power of purpose

Do you drift into the day or move into it purposefully? Are you like a dinghy adrift in a never ending ocean or like a power boat cutting through the waves to your destination? Scott Alexander in his book 'Rhinoceros Success',[1] compares a cud-chewing cow to a charging rhinoceros.

In my first book 'Why Wasn't I Told?',[2] I listed 28 main reasons why people fail to achieve what they want in life. Number one on that list is 'because they lack a strong purpose for their life'.

If you have no purpose, you have no power.

Dig the foundations deep

So purpose, I believe, is the place to start. Although we might not easily identify our purpose for life immediately, we must challenge ourselves to a first attempt. Purpose provides the framework within which our goals can be organised and prioritised. It gives us guidelines and boundaries in which to work.

> ## Purpose is like the concrete foundation we lay before building ourselves a house to live in.

We don't erect the framework until the foundation is rock solid.

But like any task that is difficult we can break it down into small bite-size pieces and tackle it one piece at a time. I call this the French breadstick method. It is very difficult to devour a 45 cm breadstick in one mouthful but easy to eat it in small bite-size chunks. Of course, this is a lot more enjoyable and comfortable too. Completing a task should be like this and just as palatable.

> ## One bite at a time and the goal is mine.

So what are the bite-size chunks that need to be attempted to help us with our purpose for living? I have devised a self-analysis questionnaire that you may find most helpful. Try writing down your answers. These could help you to uncover any hidden motives you might have for various areas of your life. I have left room for you to write down your answers immediately. Don't procrastinate! I suggest you use a pencil.

1. **State your reason(s) for working where you do.**

   _____

   _____

   _____

2. **State your reason(s) for choosing the work you do.**

   _____

   _____

   _____

3. **If you won a million dollars what changes would you make in your life?**

   _____

   _____

   _____

4. **What is your purpose for being single, married or in a partnership arrangement?**

_____

_____

_____

5. **State the reason(s) for the closeness in your family (or the lack of closeness).**

_____

_____

_____

6. **State your reason(s) for your current fitness program (or lack of).**

_____

_____

_____

Muscles: Use them or lose them

7. State your reason(s) for your current state of health and diet.

_____

_____

_____

8. If you found out today that you had only 6 months to live, what would you change in your life? (Some people have told me they would ask for half of their car insurance back.)

_____

_____

_____

9. Why have you chosen to be in your current financial situation?

_____

_____

_____

10. Why have you chosen to have the number of friends you do?

_____

_____

_____

11. State your reason(s) for your current social program or lack of.

_____

_____

_____

12. State your reason(s) for having (or not having) a family.

_____

_____

_____

13. State your reason(s) for your current belief system or lack of. (Example: Why do you believe in God, or why don't you, and on what basis have you made your decision?)

_____

_____

_____

14. Why have you chosen to spend time reading and learning each day?

_____

_____

_____

15. If you were guaranteed $100,000 per year for doing your job plus two hours reading per day, what would you read about, and why?

_____

_____

_____

Readers are leaders.

16. State your reason(s) for being involved (or not being involved) in the improvement of your community.

_____

_____

_____

17. State your reason(s) for your general level of daily happiness (or lack of).

_____

_____

_____

'If you don't believe it's a great day, just try missing one'
— Zig Ziglar.

18. **State your reason(s) for your positive and optimistic attitude to the future (or lack of).**

_____

_____

_____

19. **State your reason(s) why you feel needed by so many or so few.**

_____

_____

_____

20. **State your reason(s) for your good or poor opinion of yourself.**

_____

_____

_____

These questions may seem tedious but many people have found that their written answers have revealed their inner thoughts to themselves.

> **'Thinking is the hardest work there is, which is probably why so few engage in it.'**
> **— Henry Ford**

What we are doing here is reviewing the past and seeing how it is affecting our current thinking. If you answer the questionnaire, no matter what you think of your answers, I congratulate you on having the courage to write them down and take an honest look at yourself. You are on the way to making your future even better than your past.

If you are one of the 95 per cent of the population who

answered in your head, I would ask you to try again. Writing the answers down forces you to state your thoughts clearly and concisely. This enables you to refer back to them and build upon them later. I suggest that you will get more out of this book if you have written answers.

Now attempt to summarise your life's purpose in a few words or short sentences. Make a note of the date too.

Give your goals purpose

Avoid conflicting goals by knowing your purpose.

Remember, purpose is a foundation on which we build the rest of our lives. It prevents us from having conflicting goals, because all goals should support and bring about the fulfilment of our purpose for life. Our goals should come as a result of our life's purpose, not the other way around. Goals give greater clarity, definition and direction to how we will achieve our life's purpose. Goals are the achievable bite-size chunks into which we break down our lives. I suggest that you will be able to identify your goals under the six general headings that follow.

Emotional
Mental
Spiritual
Physical
Social
Financial

I would like to elaborate on each of these categories and share my understanding of how each heading can be used as a smaller framework within the greater framework of purpose. You can compare this process to the large family picture frames which encompass six to ten smaller pictures in the one frame. Each has a role to play in the overall picture. If the purpose of this photo display is to remind the family that they are a united, loving force, then you would leave out pictures of past boyfriends and girl-friends who are no longer part of this committed family unit. Instead, you'd include a picture of each person who is an active participant in the family team. In the same way, we identify the categories which are an integral part of our lives, but under the same all-encompassing purpose.

Emotional

This category includes any spheres of our life which heavily affect our emotions. Family goals are included here as well as goals relating to close personal relationships, such as a life partner. Goals involving compassionate causes or people in need would also fit in.

> **God doesn't look at how much we do, but with how much love we do it.'**
> **— Mother Theresa**

Try to write down two goals concerning these areas in your life.

_____

_____

_____

_____

Mental

Mental means 'to do with our learning capabilities' so this category includes goals that involve increasing and developing our knowledge. Maybe you desire to do further studies, short courses, attend seminars or adult education classes. Perhaps it is simply a goal to read better or to read more on a specific topic. Maybe you would like to improve your memory or increase your creative thinking skills.

Don't major in minors. Learn about things that count.

Some people need problem-solving skills. It is apparent that those who can assist to solve other people's problems are highly respected and often highly rewarded. Doctors get paid to solve our health problems while lawyers get paid to solve our legal problems. Teachers are trained to solve our learning problems and financial consultants are there to solve our money problems. Do you assist others to solve their problems? Before doing so we usually need to learn how to solve and cope with our own problems.

Whatever goals you select, we all need goals to expand our mental capabilities. Can you list two goals for yourself below?

_____

_____

_____

_____

Spiritual

When I write of spiritual goals some people immediately reject the idea of needing these or confuse spiritual goals with religion. Many want to skip over this category as fast as possible. Please take a minute to consider that without personal, spiritual development we leave our lives in a state of imbalance. Dr Wayne Dyer, one of the most highly respected psychologists of our time has this to say:

> **'We are not human beings who occasionally have a spiritual experience. We are spiritual beings having a human experience.'**

'Onc per cent of my humanity is form (i.e. body) while 99 per cent is spirit. It is invisible, untouchable and unsmellable. It is impervious to the senses . . . When we disassociate with the astral part of ourselves we have the true meaning of the word disaster.'

For those who say, 'But I've got religion,' I remind you of the Biblical meaning of religion. James, the brother of Jesus, wrote to all God's people scattered over the whole world and said, 'What the Father considers to be pure and genuine religion is this: to take care of orphans and widows in their suffering and to keep oneself from being corrupted by the world.' After reading this I realised that some people practise ritual instead of religion. I have been caught in this trap.

> **'Take the attitude of a student. Never be too big to ask questions. Never know too much to learn something new.'**
> **Og Mandino**

Hence, we all have a need for spiritual goals, whether they be goals to draw closer to the Lord and learn more about Him or goals to change the way we practise our religion. Some prefer to strive for more loving behaviour while others desire to develop deeper faith. Whatever you choose, you will find that the achievement of your spiritual goals will play an integral part in your overall personal growth. Attempt to list two spiritual goals immediately.

_____

_____

_____

Physical

Physical goals usually need the least explanation. They involve our fitness level, our regular diet, our posture, our hygiene, our sport and recreation. They also include our appearance, our personal habits and our speech. An important step in being successful is to look successful.

Faith it till you make it!

List two physical goals for yourself.

_____

_____

_____

_____

Social

S ocial goals are just as they sound. They include the people we meet fleetingly and those with whom we spend quality time. Included should be some goals to improve our own social skills. This could encompass goals for the clubs we join, the hobbies we do with others and the sporting teams in which we participate. In fact, wherever we are meeting and dealing with people, social goals are most helpful. They may also affect the holidays we plan. Maybe your two social goals could involve improving your manners, or being less judgemental and more forgiving. Write down two social goals now.

_____

_____

_____

_____

Financial

F inancial goals are also self-explanatory. These goals include the way we manage money, spend money, invest money and waste money. All goals to do with material possessions fit in here, but so might holidays which need to be saved for and further education courses.

List two financial goals.

_____

_____

_____

_____

'Money doesn't make the man; the man makes money!'

Do-it-yourself goal-setting

Below I have listed 12 specific areas in which I have currently set goals. Try to pick 12 priority areas in which you know you would like to have written goals.

Me	You
1. marriage (emotional goal)	1.
2. child raising (emotional goal)	2.
3. personal improvements (physical)	3.

4. health and fitness   4.
   (physical)

5. more committed friendships 5.
   (social)

6. a closer walk with God   6.
   (spiritual)

7. increasing financial wealth 7.
   (financial)

8. sharing wealth with others 8.
   (financial)

9. increasing my knowledge of 9.
   human performance and
   achievements
   (mental)

10. spreading the Good News   10.
    (spiritual)

11. positively affecting 1 million 11.
    youth
    (mental, emotional and
    spiritual)

12. places to travel   12.
    (financial and social)

People with purpose

> ## 'If you know what and why, you can work out how.'

O ur purpose and our goals are the foundations from which we derive our motivation. In this book my aim is to help you build this foundation and reinforce it in your daily life. You may gain inspiration, as I have, from some other people's experiences. Each of the following stories have deeply influenced my desire to know my own purpose and goals.

Dr Victor Frankl — In search of meaning

V ictor Frankl was a psychiatrist who was imprisoned in a German concentration camp for the last 4 years of World War II. He wrote[3] of his horrific experiences and why he survived this ordeal when thousands of others died. Although he had everything taken away from him, such as his possessions, his home, his clothes, his work, his writing and his freedom of choice, there was something they could not take. They could not take away his thoughts. He could choose what to think about and how to think about it. Even when his food, his health and his dignity were taken away and they forced him to work building roads in snow, ice and mud while chained to other prisoners he could still choose his thoughts. He could choose to hate the guards, or he could choose to feel sorry for them. He could choose to loathe his fellow prisoners (who looked like the walking dead) or he could choose to respect and comfort them. He could choose to think about his home and his past life or choose to think about how to survive where he was. He could choose to think about his future such as when he would be released or choose to give up on his life and die like so many others. Every waking minute of every day he could choose his thoughts for that moment. He couldn't choose his thoughts for tomorrow or for next week or next month. He could not even choose them for the coming evening. He could only choose his thoughts for that one moment.

While observing this in himself and others he realised one thing. Those with a purpose lived and those without a purpose died. For some, their purpose was revenge. For others it was a struggle through to freedom. Many decided to simply trust God while for others, it was their deep longing to see their family or their homeland if their families were dead. As long as they knew *why* they wanted to survive, somehow through almost impossible conditions of degradation and depravity, they would keep on living.

I compared my life with Victor Frankl's and realised that I too could choose my future. I could live life as I see so many — like the living dead. Yes, they eat, breath and sleep but their purpose is dead. They are not in a grave yet, but the rut they live in resembles one.

> ## The only difference between a grave and a rut is that a rut has the ends kicked out.

So I made my first goal to write down a purpose for my life and refine it as I went along. It was a major turning point in my life. It was the simple realisation that if I knew **what** I wanted and **why** I wanted it, the **how** to achieve it would unfold before me each day. Up to that point I had only set goals for which I knew the **how** and so limited myself to little goals, little achievements, little desires, little excitement, and little motivation.

The Miracle Man[4]

Just recently, I addressed 4000 people at a weekend conference when onto the stage walked a man whom I thought I recognised, at least by name if not by sight. The master of ceremonies said he had been in a light aircraft accident in 1981 and was hauled out of the wreckage with his back broken at the first and second vertebrae. His lungs weren't functioning nor was much else. On examination the doctors told his wife he would never walk, talk or eat again, nor breathe without a respirator. In fact he would never sit, nor use his arms or move his body. The only thing he could do was blink his eyes. If he lived, which the doctors doubted, he'd have a short unproductive life. It was a miracle that he was even alive.

Nearly 9 months later this man walked out of the hospital, breathing unaided and said goodbye to all who had nursed him. The medical staff called Morris Goodman the 'Miracle Man'. He said he recovered because of his belief in himself, his faith in God, his goal-setting and his visualising of success.

What we can conceive and believe, we can achieve.

His amazing real life story is told in a book and on an inspiring video and continues to speak for Morris in business conventions around the world. Today, Morris lives with ongoing pain as his constant companion. This pain turns to excruciating agony if he has the slightest slip, as he did the day we met.

After meeting Morris I thought of how I complained when I had a headache, and my loss of concentration if I had stomach cramps. Yet this man travels the world in constant pain encouraging hundreds of thousands of other people to do more with their lives, serve others lovingly and build a relationship with Christ.

The doctors had told him that he should just accept his situation and learn to live with it. He told them, 'The day I believe you is the day I die!'

We too, have to stop listening to the negative people in our lives. It is time to develop more love, hope, faith and goals!

The Goads — A time to live[5]

Jack and Martha Goad and their seven kids were a family of singers. The parents had dedicated their lives to raising children of strong Christian faith and high standards of service to others. One day they had all been singing in a church in a nearby town 60 miles away and on the way home their lives were turned inside out. Only 15 minutes from home Jack had a brain aneurism and ran their navy and white Dodge off the road. As 18-year-old Tim dragged himself from the wreck his older sister, Ruth, called out in terror, 'Where is Mum and Carol?' (Carol was their 6-year-old sister.)

After scanning the freeway he found the body of his little sister in a pool of glass and blood. Franctically he searched the carnage for his mother. Finally, many metres away from the van he found what he had thought to be an equipment case, but instead it was the bloodied body of his mother hidden partially by her new fur coat. He couldn't believe that she was dead.

At this point Ruth and Tim stood sobbing together in the middle of the freeway and prayed. In their distress and incomprehension they remembered their parent's teachings and prayed. 'Jesus, we don't understand why this has happened but we know that we are to give thanks to you in all circumstances and we do that now. Use this situation for your glory.' Their parents had taught them that their security was not in anything they could lose. (I wondered what type of parental teaching most kids remembered when they were in trouble.)

The Goad children went on to become one of the most successful Christian rock bands in the USA. In 1988, they performed to 4000 Australians and sang these words:

> *'You know a man who walks by the side of the road can turn himself around.*

> *'He can pick himself up, dust himself off and start all over again.'*

Maybe the time for you to start again is **now**!

Are you a 'gonna' or a goal-setter?

It's tough at the top but the view is worth it.

I hope by now you have decided upon a purpose, a framework in which to plan and build your life. Now it is time to paint more detail into the picture by way of specific goals.

- Goals are something you want to do or be or have. Goals need to be concise and specific.

- Goals must be written in the present tense, e.g. 'I am motivating myself daily by reading my goals.'
- Goals need a time target, e.g. 'I am motivating myself daily by reading my goals each morning for 21 days.'
- Goals need to paint a mental picture in your mind and conjure up feelings which will invoke action. When reading your goal you want to be able to see yourself carrying it out with enjoyment and satisfaction.
- Goals need to be said aloud with confidence as often as possible. It helps to hear yourself affirm your goals.

'What's in it for me?'

(Tune into radio station WII-FM!)

Goals need a list of personal benefits to support them. In other words you need to know 'what's in it for me' if you do work towards the goal and achieve it. It is knowing the benefits that builds desire. I suggest you write out a minimum of 20 benefits for each goal you list.

Knowing the benefits builds desire.

For example, the list of benefits for the goal below might be as follows.

'I am motivating myself daily by reading my goals each morning for 21 days.'

The benefits are:

1. I feel good when I focus on my major goals.
2. It helps to prioritise my 'To Do' list each day.
3. I feel more directed and organised.
4. It prevents me from getting bogged down by unimportant activities.
5. It prevents me from wasting time.
6. It helps me to organise myself at work and at home, as well as with the family and friends.
7. It motivates me to discipline myself.
8. It motivates me to act rather than procrastinate.
9. Others learn by my example.
10. I remain calm and unruffled more often.

11. I am achieving my goals more quickly.
12. I feel satisfied with knowing my future path.
13. I will be more easily able to incorporate new possibilities into my plan.
14. I will search for new ideas to complement my goals.
15. It decreases the possibility of depression.
16. I will gather more friends around me who will support my goals.
17. I will create an environment which supports me in my goals.
18. I will be willing to listen to the experience of others who have already enjoyed the benefits of goal-setting.
19. I will search out books and articles which will support me in my pursuits.
20. I will search out video and audio materials to assist me in achieving my goals.

The all-consuming fire of desire

Knowing the benefits can create a burning desire within you to pursue and persevere with your goals. Recent research underlines the importance of *desire*. It is the major ingredient for goal achievement. Some people have incorrectly thought that intelligence or wealth are the keys to success. Others believe that natural talent or ability is what we need. Not so. More often than not, those who achieve their goals have neither superior intelligence nor wealth. They are not blessed with unusually special talents or abilities. They achieve their goals through sheer determination, perseverance and focus. These qualities are summed up in the word *desire*. It is not wishful thinking or hoping. It is burning desire. One of my favourite sayings is this:

'There are no great people just ordinary people with great desire.'

Have you read the life stories of any of these well known people who attribute their success to desire? They all had a strong desire to do something specific with their lives.

Helen Keller
Paul McNamee
Cliff Richard
Martin Luther King
Dennis Lillee
Tom Peters
Bob Ansett
Darryl Somers
Dr Ainslie Meares
Bill Cosby

Burning desire works for the man and woman in the street too. After my seminars there are usually some people who wish to share their personal stories with me. Occasionally I meet an individual with an amazing story of triumph over tragedy. One such lady I have met was 19-year-old Kathy (not her real name). Three years previously she was diagnosed as having Hodgkin's Disease (or cancer) and doctors predicted that she would be dead within a year. A year later she lay on a hospital operating table and was declared dead. She had an out-of-body experience but returned to tell the story. Today she says that her desire to live is immense. This fuelled her desire to turn the tables on her school career. After being known as a low achiever for 10 years of school life, she set out to be an A grade student in Year 11. To the amazement of her teachers and friends, she did exactly that. Then Kathy decided to get involved with a cancer support group for teenagers called Canteen. She has watched many of her friends pass away. At eighteen and a half years old her father died of cancer. At nineteen years old her sister dropped dead from a blood clot in the lungs. Kathy copes through her determination and her ability to move on and help others. She says, 'I must be alive for a reason. Now I am looking for that reason.'

Two weeks after her sister's death Kathy befriended a beautiful 17-year-old girl at a Canteen camp. Not only did she offer her friendship, but she patiently taught her new friend Sally to make a six-strand friendship bracelet, ride a horse, roller skate, paddle a canoe and jet ski. And Kathy did it with absolute joy and pleasure. This would not seem unusual except that her friend Sally is blind. If you ask Kathy who gets the most out of her new friendship she won't hesitate as she admits that she does.

So what next awaits this motivated teenager? Kathy says she want to inspire Australian teenagers to achieve more with their lives. That is desire! She wants to do more than keep on keeping on.

The French breadstick method

Once you have got your written goal and a host of reasons why you should achieve it, the next step is to make a game plan. With your desire level running high you must map out a way to break down your goal into bite size chunks.

You can compare this process to a football game or tennis match. Professional sports people play each game with a goal and a desire to win. However, they usually have a pre-planned strategy for how they will achieve this goal, step by step. Although they often don't know their opposition's strategy nor their level of performance on that particular day, they plan for what they do know and add to their plan as the game progresses. We must do the same. So begin to work out some simple starting steps for each of your goals.

Bite by bite the load is light.

Obstacles and other problems

For every goal we have there will always be obstacles on our way to its achievement. In a football game, it is called 'opposition'. It is your attitude to obstacles that will determine how long the obstacle remains a barrier between you and your goal.

I have a sign on one of my walls that says, **'If you're not part of the solution, then you're part of the problem.'** This reminds me to begin working on solutions immediately. Every day I delay only builds the barrier higher (at least in my mind). Obstacles can be anticipated and planned for.

- Obstacles need to be recognised, not denied.
- Obstacles are to be overcome, not overlooked.
- Obstacles should be welcomed, not feared.
- Obstacles make you stronger, not weaker.
- Obstacles should build character, not complaints.
- Obstacles should make us better, not bitter.
- Obstacles are an integral part of the challenge of life.

James Allen, author of 'As A Man Thinketh . . .' says that circumstances do not make a man, they reveal him. Kathy had no choice in her circumstances or her obstacles, but she certainly could choose how she reacted to them.

Obstacles are goals in disguise!

Enthuse or diffuse

'Nothing great was ever achieved without enthusiasm,' wrote Ralph Waldo Emerson, one of the great thinkers of our time.

'A man can succeed at almost anything for which he has unlimited enthusiasm,' said Charles M. Schwob, one of the greatest American industrialists.

Henry Thoreau, one of the greatest philosophers of this century, said 'None are so old as those who have outlived enthusiasm.'

Norman Vincent Peale, famous author and preacher stated that the Bible has this to say about enthusiasm: 'Be renewed in the spirit of your mind,' and, 'Walk in newness of Life.' In other words, don't allow your mind to fill with misery, indifference or boredom. Fill it with enthusiasm.

'Life is either a daring adventure or nothing,' believed Helen Keller, the woman who was born deaf, dumb and blind and went on to become one of the world's most admired women.

> **'Life is either a daring adventure or nothing.'**
> **— Helen Keller**

William James proposes that we use the 'act as if principle'. If you are sad and you no longer want to be sad, act as if you were happy. That means, put a smile on your face, organise to see a friend, think of fun things to say and do enjoyable activities. If you persevere with acting as if you were happy, it won't be long before you will be. Consider the question of whether you sing because you are happy or are happy because you sing.

If you are not receiving the promotion you believe you have earned, being miserable won't help. You will only confirm the boss's decision. If you act as if you are getting a promotion, then it is likely that you will.

Famous author Dale Carnegie, who wrote 'How to Win Friends and Influence People',[6] said that 'we learn by doing'. If this is so, and I believe it is, you won't know if enthusiasm works until you try it out for yourself.

How to handle negative people and situations

Charlie Jarvis, a famous humourist, says, 'There are not many negative people in the world. They are probably as few as 10 per cent of the population, but that 10 per cent seem to get around a lot.'

Do you know any negative people? They are the ones who look like they have been weaned on a lemon. They have always got a sour face. Other people seem to cheer up when they leave the room.

Three simple steps to avoid criticism — say nothing, do nothing, be nothing.

Negative people come in many different disguises. First there are the Whingers. They always find something to complain about. Some even blame it on the fact that they were born upside down! They wished they had had a chance to put their feet on the ground first. You will hear them say things like, 'It's too hot!' or 'I can't do it!' or 'It's not fair' or 'Why do I have to do it?'

The second group are the Cynics. They believe nothing good about anyone or anything. They rarely give people the benefit of the doubt. Their comments are often cutting and highly critical. If someone succeeds in their place of work they are the first ones to accuse them of devious means or foul play.

Thirdly, we have the Gossips. They choose the 'spicy untruths' in preference to the truth so as to bring attention to themselves. They have to be the bearers of bad news because they are usually guaranteed a reaction which fuels their gossip. People who gossip often need to be ignored and told why.

There is only one way to deal with negative people, even when the atmosphere is thick with accusation. I want to emphasise the following statement.

> ### 'Don't allow other people to decide your mood for the day.'

At all times one person influences another. It is up to you whether you decide to influence or be influenced. No-one can make you mad without you first giving them permission to do so.

Just as Victor Frankl discovered, 'When your world collapses around you you can still choose your thoughts.' To blame another for your bad moods is to relinquish responsibility for your thoughts and actions. It is like giving over the steering wheel of your life to another. If you want to control your own moods, keep your hands firmly on your own wheel.

What is your environment like?

When was the last time you really felt motivated? Where were you? Whom were you with? What were the surroundings? What were you doing? What were you thinking? What were you motivated about? How were you feeling? Jot some notes below.

_____

_____

_____

Try to recall some of these moments right now. Do you think that the environment affects your level of motivation? Make a list of people who inspire you. Then make a list of the people who you inspire.

_____

_____

_____

_____

_____

Why do you feel motivated around certain people? Make a note of how often you see them. Do you think you should plan to see them more regularly? Yes, we do become like the people we spend most of our time with. It is important to choose your friends carefully and choose how we spend that time with them. For example, if you go to the movies do you choose movies that leave you uplifted, or drained and depressed? Can you write a list of inspiring and uplifting movies? Would you ever think of viewing them again when feeling low?

Which songs really uplift you? Have you made a tape of songs that really get you going when you need it? Or do you leave your moods to chance?

What type of scenery calms you? Beaches, lakes, rivers, mountains, parks, gardens, farms, orchards, factories, cities, suburbia, shops, high-rise buildings, crowds of people, libraries, hospitals? Know how these environments affect you and use this information to your advantage.

Sometimes the most important thing you can do is take a complete rest.

Peace starts at home

Is your home a place of inspiration? If world peace begins at home, what is your place like?

You don't need an expensive or luxurious home to make it inspirational. It is the way we decorate it that counts. I have chosen to cover my walls with beautiful scenic pictures with positive or inspiring quotes on them. They are uplifting to read and enticing to the eye. What do you see, day in and day out, on your walls? Do you have at least one room which is an inspiration to be in? Some people even make it the toilet or the bathroom. (My bathroom is plastered with 36 pages of goals, quotes and inspiring Bible passages.) Is your home decorated for your benefit and enjoyment or for what others might think of you? No-one would call my bathroom beautiful, but my guests spend hours in there reading all my hand-written pages. But, most importantly, I read them every morning and evening to keep my thoughts on the subjects I want them to dwell.

Obstacles are what you see when you take your eyes off your goals.

Have you got a goal board in your home? It can be just a simple cork board on which you pin up all your goals and pictures of things you would like to own. When I was overweight after an overseas trip, I stuck an attractive trim body without the head, on my bathroom mirror and told myself it was me. It reminded me that the weight and shape and fitness of my body was my responsibility and choice. Of course, I couldn't change my bone structure or basic shape, but I could make the most of what God had given me. What are you doing about keeping your body in the shape you want it?

The goal board

The goal board has also helped me to spend my money more wisely. Instead of spontaneously buying an item I saw and liked, it helped to mentally remind me of my priorities. I could weigh up the new enticing item I was looking at, against those items on the board. Some items I have listed on a card in my wallet. 'What did I really want to invest my money in first?' I would ask myself. It helped me to make better buying decisions. I remember weighing up a new silk dress versus saving for a holiday in Cairns I had pictured. I decided I would rather 'do it' than 'wear it'. From that day on I often chose to spend my money on activities and experiences rather than clothes, furniture and other possessions. Make some decisions about where your preferences lay. Prioritise the list below but add some of your own categories first. At least know your 'top ten' money expenditure categories in the order you see them as important in your life.

- ☐ annual holidays
- ☐ home improvements
- ☐ clothes
- ☐ eating out
- ☐ day excursions
- ☐ children's education
- ☐ self-improvement education
- ☐ gifts for family and friends
- ☐ jewellery
- ☐ furniture
- ☐ charities
- ☐ study courses/further education
- ☐ music/TV/video
- ☐ entertainment
- ☐ sporting equipment
- ☐ church donations
- ☐ weekends away
- ☐ luxury foods
- ☐ hobbies
- ☐ artwork
- ☐ hair and beauty treatments
- ☐ health foods
- ☐ gym membership, massages, stress courses

Believe it till you achieve it.

Do you think ahead?

Plan for the inevitable, not the improbable.

Your motivation is affected by many factors. Primarily it is your thoughts that count most. Then comes your activities, your feelings, people, surroundings and so on (not necessarily in that order). Most of the ideal circumstances for you to **feel** motivated don't come about by chance. They need planning and organisation. If you just wait until you **feel** motivated, you could be waiting a long time. Some people do this with their spiritual development. They wait for the day they **feel** they need it. Unfortunately, this usually comes with the death of a loved one or deep personal depression. They can find no comfort in their beliefs at these times because they have not yet sought to understand the mysteries of faith, hope and eternal life. Motivation, like faith, must not depend on your feelings. Feelings are unreliable and down right erratic. They can change suddenly and erratically or slowly and insidiously. Feelings fluctuate because of your diet and nutrition, energy level, exercise program (or lack of it), family problems, loneliness, relationship problems, job, body hormones, difficulties, the weather, careless comments by friends, music, movies, news and scenery.

Are you really going to wait until all these factors are perfect in your life and then hope you will feel like doing something. Of course not. Feelings are fickle! Don't run your life by them. Make choices and make plans. The Bible says in Proverbs, Chapter 4:

> **'Plan carefully what you do and what you plan will turn out right.'**

Know which activities make you feel most content or at peace. Tick any below that help you to achieve a peaceful state of mind and add others that you know are useful to you in difficult times.

☐ walking	☐ dancing	☐ fixing
☐ running	☐ aerobics	☐ writing
☐ swimming	☐ gardening	☐ photography
☐ sailing	☐ painting	☐ singing
☐ riding	☐ creating	☐ laughing
☐ flying	☐ building	☐ telling jokes
☐ skiing	☐ designing	☐ praying
☐ skating	☐ sewing	☐ meditating
☐ climbing	☐ cooking	☐ thinking

_____

_____

_____

How to feel important

Feeling important, needed and loved is also an integral part of successful living. Know which activities make you feel this way by perusing the list below and ticking those that apply to you. Feel free to add to this list also.

☐ teaching/instructing others
☐ helping
☐ holding a child
☐ speaking to groups
☐ being seen at an important social occasion
☐ training for a sport
☐ seeing your picture in the paper
☐ chatting to friends
☐ assisting an elderly person
☐ caring for a child
☐ drinking alcohol
☐ smoking
☐ holding a loved one
☐ healing others
☐ being thankful
☐ praising God
☐ living enthusiastically
☐ simply being yourself

How often do you schedule these activities into your life? Select the ones you would like to add to your life and cross out the ones you would like to eliminate from your life. Remember, that doing is better than just reading.

Thoughts to cultivate

What do you spend most of your time thinking about. The psychologists say we live 80 per cent of our lives in our minds. Does that mean that we spend 80 per cent of our thinking or living time thinking about things that will never happen? Mind activity includes day dreaming, night dreaming, fantasising, hoping, worrying, fearing, wondering, contemplating, meditating, praying. This doesn't mean that these things are all useless but they do take up a lot of time. It would be more useful to change worrying to problem solving and fearing to fact finding and faith.

Fear and faith cannot both exist in the mind at the same time.

Worry and fear are pretty useless. Being concerned and taking action is more appropriate.

As for day dreaming, it is part of the process for envisioning the future. It is a good idea not to do it when focus and concentration are required. Hope is much the same. We need hope for the future, but what we hope for often requires **action**.

Be prepared to take action.

Night dreaming and fantasising are too big a topic to tackle in this book. Wondering and contemplating mean thinking and we need a lot of both. Meditating and praying are focused forms of thinking. For prayer, we choose specific topics to talk to God about, such as family well being, healing and personal growth. Meditation on the other hand is not a conversation with God but rather a dwelling on a specific verse of scripture, such as 'Love one another', or dwelling on a wise saying, or an inspiring poem. For some it is allowing words to sink into conscious understanding or alpha brain level. For others it is trying to remove all thoughts from the mind.

So on what does all your thought power get expended? The Bible has some very specific advice on thinking.

Prov. 4:23
Be careful how you think. Your life is *shaped by your thoughts*.
Prov. 3:5-7
. . . Never rely on what you think you know. Remember the Lord in everything you do and He will show you the right way. *Never let yourself think that you are wiser than you are*
Philippians 6:8 (in my words)
Don't worry about anything. In everything, *be thankful* and pray and ask God for what you want.
Whatever is true, noble, right and pure, whatever is lovely or admirable. If anything is excellent or praiseworthy think about such things and put it into practice . . . And the God of peace will be with you.

> ## In other words, fill your mind with all that is good and rid yourself of negative thinking.

How to talk yourself into success

When I speak to youth rallies around Australia I often try to explain the concept of self-talk. We all know we talk to ourselves but we often don't know where the thoughts and ideas come from. Why do some have happy thoughts most of the time while others seem continually miserable? Many comparisons are made between the computer and the mind. The similarity lies in the fact that whatever information is put into a computer also comes out.

> ## If you put garbage in you get garbage out.

No more, no less. Therefore if you learn just 'the good stuff' all your thoughts are good. But let me give you some idea of how clever your brain is. Imagine a telephone switchboard that fills up 50 floors of office space. You are in control of this switchboard and you can ring anywhere in the world. But not only that, you can speak to millions of different people in different countries at the same time. Simultaneously millions of people in every country with telephones can ring you. You have billions of phone calls operating at the same time and all information being retained and stored for when you need it. That is what your brain does for your body. It talks to billions of cells at the same time as billions of other cells are sending information up to the brain. What a magnificent computer! So keep putting in the good stuff! But there is a problem here. Have you ever had an awful nightmare or bad thought that you have never read about, heard about, seen or experienced? If you have, you can join the rest of the population in this common experience. But what about this one? Have you ever had a great idea or a beautiful dream without ever having read about it, heard about it, seen it or experienced it? I hope you have! So what does this prove, you might be asking. Well, it proves your brain is more than a computer.

It proves that somewhere, somehow, other information is being put into your mind. I call it the secret three-way conversation. The best way I have found to describe it, in simple terms, is the following.

Imagine that on your left shoulder is sitting a little fellow with a megaphone in his hand. He is wearing a black suit, a black shirt and a black tie. In fact, everything is black and he is holding a little pitchfork. He looks bad, mean and nasty. We call him the devil's helper or Mr C. E. Ville.

On your right shoulder is sitting another little fellow, but he is all in white. In fact he is shining all the time, even in the dark. He holds no megaphone, no pitchfork, just a book. He looks lovable, gentle and caring. We call him God's messenger or Mr U. R. Good.

Your thoughts make you or break you.

Now Mr C. E. Ville and Mr U. R. Good never agree on anything. They talk to you all the time and give you conflicting views on yourself and everything else.

Mr U. R. Good thinks you are a winner.

Mr C. E. Ville insists you are a loser.

Mr U. R. Good thinks you are a leader.

Mr C. E. Ville insists you are a wimp.

Mr U. R. Good believes that you are one of a kind, you are special.

Mr C. E. Ville screams that you are just like everyone else.

Mr U. R. Good believes that you are on your way to victory.

Mr C. E. Ville screams that you are on your way to misery.

Mr U. R. Good thinks you will achieve great things through your faith.

Mr C. E. Ville insists you will probably die poor, depressed and lonely.

Mr U. R. Good believes you are a person of quality and character.

Mr C. E. Ville insists you are just an overrated animal.

Mr U. R. Good knows that you can be eternally happy.

Mr C. E. Ville tricks you to believe that what you cannot see does not exist.

Mr U. R. Good knows that you are lovable.

Mr C. E. Ville implies that you are not.

Mr U. R. Good gives good practical advice.

Mr C. E. Ville tries to confuse your thinking.

Mr U. R. Good helps you out of tricky spats.

Mr C. E. Ville helps you into them.

Mr U. R. Good helps you to serve others.

Mr C. E. Ville tells you to take care of no. 1.

Mr U. R. Good gives you dreams and visions.

Mr C. E. Ville gives you worry and despair.

So the question of great importance is . . . which one are you going to listen to? Not only do you need to put good positive input into your mind, you also need to tune out the negative thoughts and ideas that just seem to pop up. I teach my seminar attendees a simple humorous method of tuning into Mr U. R. Good and tuning out to Mr C. E. Ville. Raise your right arm in the air with your palm forward. Bend it at the elbow and give yourself four firm pats on the left shoulder. Guess what you just did? You squashed Mr C. E. Ville or at least silenced him for a while. (You can smile now!) And every time you get a negative thought, that is an easy way to remind yourself that who you listen to is *your choice*. And while you are giving yourself a pat on the back, don't forget to give someone else one too! Happy Living!

References

1. Published by The Rhino's Press Inc., 1987.
2. Published by Cassette Learning Systems, 1986.
3. Victor Frankl, *Man's Search for Meaning*, 3rd edn, Simon & Schuster Inc., 1984.
4. Morris Goodman & Pat Garnett, *The Miracle Man*, Prentice Hall Inc., 1985.
5. Doug Wead, *A Time To Live*, Restoration Fellowship, 1982.
6. Published by Eden Paperbacks, revised edn, 1984.

Daniel Johnson is an international authority on time management and self-organization. Well known author of over 200 published articles and the book 'How to Win the Paper War', Daniel is in constant demand as a keynote speaker to share his motivating techniques and practical know how.

PART

2

HOW TO
Manage
YOURSELF

by
Daniel Johnson

Build your energy reserves

'Don't serve time, make time serve you.'
— Willie Sutton

Value your time

Over the past five years I have surveyed literally thousands of seminar participants and asked them to define time. It's a measure, it is the sequence of events, it's something we cannot waste, a precious resource etc. . . . These are popular responses but the most frequent answer of all is: time is money. It is a commonly accepted definition but is it the best one?

You can make money, save money, spend money, and even give it away, can't you? In contrast there is only one thing you can do with your time: spend it. Your time can never be replaced. Once it's spent it's gone forever.

The best definition of time which conveys it's true importance is: **time is life!** After agreeing to this definition you will never 'kill time' again because the next time you are just 'killing time' waiting for an appointment or a long-winded friend to finish their story you'll say to yourself, 'I am not killing time, I'm killing my life!'

With this new attitude comes new levels of energy and a new zest for life.

> **'Doest thou love life? Then do not squander time; for that's the stuff life is made of.'**
> **— Benjamin Franklin**

Just think about it for a moment. What's the best use of your life on a weekday evening? Is it watching televison or is it building your own business or is it learning to play the flute or is it sharing quality time with your family? The decision is yours because this is your life!

The best use of my time on a weekday evening is:

_____

_____

_____

Think about why you do what you do.

Use the power of positive self-talk

There is nothing in life that drains energy from a person more than negative emotions and thoughts. Unfortunately we live in a society of predominantly negative feedback. The media reports overwhelmingly negative news, parents are frequently negative (for example that all too frequent statement, 'Don't do that!'), and you probably hear more from your boss about what you've done wrong than what you've done right.

To counter those negative external inputs requires constant positive self-talk which builds you up, generates excitement, confidence and enthusiasm. For example, let's say you wish to run a 42 km marathon race and you've never done it before. As you train day after day building up your fitness, you could, as most do, let your mind wander onto any subject (which is likely to be, 'Why the heck am I doing this?' or 'Oh, my legs ache'). There is a better approach.

> ## 'Act enthusiastic and you become enthusiastic.' — Dale Carnegie

Manage yourself and fill your mind with positive affirmations while you run, such as, 'I am fit and a strong three and one-half hours finisher in the marathon.' Breaking down this example demonstrates the ten essential elements of positive affirmations:

1. Use the **first person** — 'I'.
2. Use the **present tense** — 'am' versus 'will'.
3. Make them **positive** — 'fit' versus 'not overweight'.
4. Use **action words** which trigger emotion — 'fit'.
5. Use **emotional words** — 'strong'.
6. Make it **specific** — 'three and one half hours'.
7. Make it **realistic** — you must believe you can achieve it.
8. Indicate **achievement** — 'finisher'.
9. Make it **accurate** — 'in the marathon'.
10. Have **balance** — this example is a fitness affirmation; also use them with family, business/income, etc.

Positive self-talk is the success secret of winners in all walks of life. Make it a part of your life from today onwards.

Invest the time right now to pick up your pen and create a positive affirmation for yourself about an area of life you wish to improve or a goal you are achieving. Once you've written it down compare it to the preceeding ten elements of a positive affirmation.

_____

_____

_____

Exercise to increase your energy

The fitness fad of the seventies is here to stay. Why? The benefits of staying healthy are so dramatic.

Some cynics suggest that by exercising regularly you will be draining yourself of energy that could be poured into other areas of life. That's true only for those who exercise to the extreme. For example, football players and Olympic athletes may drain themselves in training and competition to such an extent they have little reserves left.

Exercise in moderation on a regular basis actually increases your energy level. Your body produces adrenalin and endorphines while exercising. The adrenalin keeps you going and the endorphines are a natural pain-killer which is believed to be 50 times more potent than morphine. In other words, modern medical research has proven the validity of the expression you have probably heard before, 'I'm high on life.'

Moderate levels of exercise improve your ability to concentrate, your clarity of thinking, and your energy levels. Create a schedule that includes at least 25 minutes of exercise three times a week and you will reap the benefits of a healthier body, a clearer mind and more vitality.

Being a professional speaker I have a very hectic schedule at times with flights every day from city to city. Seminar participants

'You have nothing to lose by "going for it".'
— Paul Hogan

Ask yourself: 'Can I afford not to exercise?'

often inquire, 'How can you possibly afford the time to exercise with such a hectic schedule?' Based on the dramatically increased levels of energy which result from exercising my response is, 'I can't afford not to exercise.'

Your next question is probably, 'Okay, that sounds fine, I agree I should exercise more but how do I find the time?' The answer is simple yet powerful. Sleep less!

Sleep less and achieve more

Just take a moment to sit back and contemplate your life. Think about what you have achieved and what you could achieve with more time and energy. Remember that time is life — your most precious resource. Would you be able to write more letters, take more photographs, study more, build your business more with an hour or two of additional time each day?

Here is another way to look at it. Joel Weldon, an American professional speaker, recalls an episode which illustrates this point clearly. Several years ago Joel was waiting in a line with several other restaurant patrons to pay his bill and leave the restaurant when a gentleman, who explained he was in a rush, asked if he could jump the queue and leave before Joel. Being an obliging young man, Joel granted this man his request but before doing so he asked this busy executive why he was in such a hurry.

The stranger explained he owned several businesses, was writing a book and leaving shortly on a trip around the world. Amazed Joel asked, 'How can you achieve so much?' The man looked back and asked Joel, 'How old are you?' Joel said, '30 years old.' The response was, 'Then you have probably been asleep for 10 years.'

That's exactly right, if you sleep the normal eight hours per night, that is one-third of your life consumed in a completely non-productive activity. Much research has been conducted which concludes that the majority of people in our society sleep more than they physically require.

> **'Whenever anything gets done by anyone it is done, I have found, by a monomaniac with a mission.' — Peter Drucker**

As a result of extensive research Dr Jim Horne of the Sleep Institute in England has come to the conclusion that the optimum amount of sleep required is five and a half to six hours per night, for the average adult.

Find more to do

Dr Horne discovered something of even more compelling interest apart from determining the optimum sleeping time. Even after the research volunteers knew their optimum sleeping time only a handful made the choice to continue sleeping less after the study was completed. Why? The vast majority did not achieve any more even though they had up to three hours of extra waking time each day. Those people found that **work expands to fill the time available**. In other words, they did not achieve more; they just kept themselves busy for longer each day.

He who hesitates sleeps his life away.

Those who reduced their sleeping time to optimum level on an ongoing basis were really the self-motivated ones. They applied the principles in this book and had the discipline and motivation to achieve more every day forever!

'Okay, that all sounds great but how do I go about it?'

Based on the experience of hundreds of seminar participants

and my own experience the key is to reduce your sleeping time gradually by waking up a little bit earlier. Continue your normal routine, going to bed at the same time as always but tomorrow morning wake up just five minutes earlier. The key is to force yourself to get out of bed that little bit earlier. Do not, under any circumstance, 'sleep in' the extra five minutes and arise at your normal time. If you do it once it will wipe out all your efforts and you are likely to slip into your old sleeping pattern quickly.

> **'Take time to think — it is the source of power. Take time to play — it is the secret of perpetual youth. Take time to read — it is the fountain of wisdom. Take time to love and be loved — it is a privilege. Take time to laugh — it is the music of the soul. Take time to give — it is too short a day to be selfish. Take time to work — it is the price of success.'**

Program your mind to wake up earlier by concentrating on two things as you lay in bed and drift off to sleep. First, think about what you will do with the extra time you will have: it might be reading, exercising, working, etc. Next, visualize yourself feeling energetic and excited as you wake up that extra little bit earlier the next morning.

Gill Moxom, a seminar participant from Melbourne, uses this idea most successfully. She enjoys reading and now devotes 15 minutes each morning to reading. Knowing that she has something special which she truly enjoys each morning is the spark that motivates her to sleep less.

Personally, having the extra time in the mornings for exercise and creative thinking is my motivator. My best writing is done in the early hours of the day before the rest of the household or the rest of the city has begun to stir. I've already set the day off to a great start.

Once you are comfortable with waking up that little bit earlier (usually after a week or two) it is time to trim another 5 or 10 minutes off your sleeping time. Remember: continue retiring at the same time in the evening so that you are actually reducing your sleeping time. Within a few months you will have found your own optimum sleeping time.

Do you wake up to an alarm or to an opportunity?

Following are a few helpful hints to sleep less:
- Move your opportunity clock (it wakes you to opportunities, verses an 'alarm clock') at least 5 metres from your bed which forces you to physically get up. Once you are halfway to the bathroom, well, what the heck, you might as well continue on, freshen up and start the day.
- Use an automatic timer which turns on a set of flood lights, a stereo and a strong fan. If you are a deep sleeper and it's the dark depths of winter then this extreme may be just what you need.
- Join a health club or exercise group which meets early in the morning. Often it is this sort of commitment to others which is the extra stimulation you need to boost yourself out of bed.

My 'spark' which will motivate me to sleep less is

_____

_____

Plan to achieve your goals

> **'Plan your work and work your plan.'**
> **— Norman Vincent Peale**

Be honest with yourself

If you want to do more, be more and achieve more, planning will play a vital role in your success. It's rare that individuals plan their life too much. In most cases it's the opposite. People feel, 'Gee, I'm afraid to plan too much because I won't be spontaneous or able to enjoy life. Even worse, what if I don't achieve my plan?'

The truth is the people who make things happen know what they want to achieve, set their goals and then lay the plans to achieve them. It is the plans which turn goals into reality.

> **'The discipline of writing something down is the first step toward making it happen.'**
> **— Lee Iacocca**

All football coaches worthy of their position never ever send a team into play without a game plan. Just imagine a team of football players running randomly around the field wanting to win but not knowing how. They could be in better physical shape and have better skills than their opponents yet still lose the game. The successful coach's plan is clearly defined but flexible; it is sure to change as the game progresses.

If you fail to plan, you plan to fail.

A game plan will increase your odds for winning just as it does for the football coach. Having a plan for each year, each week and each day generates excitement in life, keeps you moving and provides that sense of direction that allows you to focus your energy on opportunities to grow and improve.

Yearly planning

Once you have your lifetime goals in place the best point to begin any sort of detailed planning is on a yearly basis. The first thing to do, especially if you are self employed or in sales, is to be honest with yourself and determine when you will not work. Set aside the holiday time in advance, even down to the weekends away.

That's right, plan ahead and hang a large yearly planning board (available at any major stationery store) on the wall and block off the holidays. Now you can see just how much time is left for work. Next, fill in any major commitments or deadlines you are aware of. These could include training courses, conferences to attend, targets to reach, birthdays, etc. Now aim to set blocks of time aside for major activities you plan to achieve. Set yourself deadlines for that short story you want to write, those books you are going to read, when you will complete painting the house, and so on.

> **'Plan for the future because that's where you are going to spend the rest of your life.'**
> **— Mark Twain**

On the yearly planner, highlight each different area of life with a different colour or symbol. For example, holidays in green, work commitments in red and committees or club meetings in blue. As you build your plan, your future will unfold before you. A planner of this nature once completed offers you a visual representation of the future. Display it where you will see it at least daily, update it as required, and in just three to four hours you will have developed your overall plan for the year.

Some of the major commitments, deadlines and items I will place on my yearly planner are:

Item   *Colour to be used*

1. _____   _____

2. _____   _____

3. _____   _____

4. _____   _____

5. _____   _____

Daily planning

The single best method of managing yourself to achieve your goals and increase your personal productivity is a powerful, tiny, easy-to-use, daily tool called the 'to do list'. On first examination the 'to do list' looks very straightforward and it really is. Interviews with hundreds of successful individuals and years of experience have revealed a few vital principles to me, which, when you apply them, will make the 'to do list' most effective for you.

Writing your list must become a daily habit. The time to formalize this list of the things you must accomplish tomorrow is during the last few minutes of today either in the afternoon at work or in the evening at home.

Good daily habits lead to lifetime success.

Below is an example plucked at random from a page in my diary:

1. Run 7 km.
4. Follow-up 3 clients.
2. Complete 6 pages of book.
5. Prepare magazine article outline.
3. Play with Yvonne and Jarvis (my children) for one hour.
6. Write letters to 4 clients.

Let's analyse this list. It is short (only six items), specific and achievable, which makes it motivating. Beware of demotivating yourself with an overwhelming list of things to be done which you know will not be achieved. Each item is a clearly defined objective. There is little detail as each acts as a reminder only.

The most important of all are the numbers which indicate the priority of each item based on its importance, the sequence of how they will be done. For example, item number three, playing with my children, would not be practical to complete in sequence on a business day.

> **'I used to keep a sign opposite my desk where I couldn't miss it. If I was on the telephone (about to make an appointment) or in a meeting in my office: "Is what I'm doing or about to do getting us closer to our objective?"' — Robert Townsend**

Here's how you tackle a 'to do list'. Always begin with the highest priority item. If you are unable for some reason to complete it at that moment move onto the next in the sequence. As you continue through the day make certain at every moment you are working on the highest priority item possible. Of course, crises or urgent requests occur. Handle them as efficiently as possible then return to your current top priority item.

Knowing your priorities takes away the pressure.

You are bound to have plenty of other reminders, phone calls to make, and 101 other tasks to complete. Keep these lower priority items on a separate list, preferably away from your 'to do list'. These items don't need to have priorities established or specific time scheduled to complete them. Just fit them in when you can, ideally after all of your top priorities have been completed.

Get started straight away with this action idea by writing your 'to do list' for tomorrow below:

Priority   *My daily goals for tomorrow*

_____   _____

_____   _____

_____   _____

_____   _____

_____   _____

Keep yourself organised

We can't manage time, but we can manage how we 'spend' it.

Focus your thinking

**'Concentration is my motto. First honesty, then industry, then concentration.'
— Andrew Carnegie**

Imagine walking into the lecture hall of a well-known university to listen to an address by the world's leading authority on your favourite subject, let's say it is Victorian architecture. You'd be expecting an informative, interesting and educational presentation. As you enter the auditorium you're extremely disappointed. On the stage next to the speaker is a group of flamingo dancers, the lighting and colours belong in a disco, waitresses are walking through the aisles handing out free beer, wine and spirits. There are TV monitors placed strategically in the hall to catch your attention. They are playing a current movie you wanted to see. Is it possible you would have just a little bit of trouble giving this world authority your full attention? Certainly. Fortunately if you were sufficiently interested, trained and disciplined you would tune your mind into the speaker and tune out all of the distractions.

You see, the conscious mind focuses effectively on only one thing at a time.

To be well organised and stay well organised all you need do is apply the concept of focusing on only one thing at a time to all areas of your life. Every organisation system from a diary to a kitchen cupboard spice rack should be designed with this underlying principle.

Uncluttering your environment unclutters your mind.

Unclutter your life

Begin with your closets and work out from there. Clean out every wardrobe, every drawer, every filing cabinet, every message book, address book, etc. you have. As you clean your environment, you begin to feel better. You are regaining control. A cluttered office, bedroom or kitchen has its own unique way of taking control of what you do.

> **'Cleaning your house while your kids are still growing is like shovelling the walk before it stops snowing.' — Phyllis Diller**

When you arrive in the morning to a disorganised mess you begin to act like a disorganised mess. The instant reaction for most office workers when they are confronted with a cluttered work environment is the thought, 'Where should I begin?' The starting point then becomes sorting through the piles. Unless the clutter is eliminated this thought process repeats itself regularly throughout the day, burning unnecessary energy and wasting time.

The basic approach to organising your clutter is to throw out all unnecessary items first, then store or file items required for possible use later in a categorised system (i.e. an A to Z filing cabinet). This will leave you with a pile of projects to be done or to be completed (i.e. letters to write, socks to mend, curtains to make, slide shows to produce . . .). Now sort through these one at a time. Do those that can be done immediately and plan when you will complete the others. You may choose to create a list of all these uncompleted projects. Once you've reached this stage . . . Congratulations! You are now on top of it all and in control of your life.

List below the major five areas of clutter in your life and the commitment to cleaning them up for the next 7 days:

Priority   *Major area of clutter*

1. _____   _____

2. _____   _____

3. _____   _____

4. _____   _____

5. _____   _____

Bring your life together with a diary

With the clutter under control it is time to turn to your diary. For the well organised individual today, a diary is no longer only an appointment book. It is a central planning and organisational tool. It is the place to combine all the different sources of personal references into one. With a good time-management diary system you have only one book to look for appointments, addresses, goals, notes, lists of things to do, projects being planned, commitments made to others, etc.

What I have just described is a ring binder system with various dividers or sections. There are several of these products on the market with various styles, features and benefits. Search for the system that suits your needs the best.

Here are two secrets to remember: Use pencil only (your plans should be flexible); and keep your diary with you at all times. As you become accustomed to using your diary for personal and business items it will become something you carry with you like a wallet or a purse. You should take it everywhere and use it frequently. No longer will you need to remember those miscellaneous details as they will all be kept in your diary, allowing you to unclutter your mind, and leaving your mind free to focus on only one thing at a time.

It's simple systems that work

The objective of personal organisation is for you to stay in control, to save time and to make managing your life as easy as possible. Therefore, when it comes to creating or selecting organisational systems make sure they are simple to use. Overly complex systems often have the disadvantage of being time-consuming.

Look for single-entry systems. One of the best examples are the small business accounting systems which have carbon-backed receipts and cheques. As you write out a receipt or cheque it is automatically recorded as a journal entry in your books. These are simple, easy-to-maintain systems that allow you to stay well organised.

'Things should be made as simple as possible but not simpler.' — Albert Einstein

Today there are some spectacular and powerful personal computer-based programs that truly take the busy work out of personal organisation. For example, for sales people these programs can provide all client information and even remind the salesperson of the people who require follow-up and for what reason. That one basic function is just the beginning of the almost limitless benefits that personal computer packages can offer.

A word of advice: Before selecting a computerised system, study the manual systems. A simple file-card system with follow-up reminders in your diary may be the most efficient and effective system for you.

Another factor which contributes to the usefulness of organisational systems is to select those which have colour codings. Many of the better filing systems have colours which correspond to numbers. For organisations with thousands of files catalogued by numbers, these systems can save huge amounts of filing time.

On an individual level, colour coding can be applied to any area which demands staying organised. One of my seminar participants from HBA, a health insurance company in Melbourne, has a spiral pad where she writes notes to herself and records any commitments she makes to other people. All of the items which require her to take action are written in red with notes and reminders recorded in blue. At a glance she is immediately aware of all of her outstanding jobs. It is simple and requires minimal extra effort, yet it allows her to be much better organised than her colleagues.

'YESTERDAY is a cancelled cheque. TOMORROW is a promissory note. TODAY is ready cash. Use it!'

Simple systems result in satisfying work.

Recommended reading list

Edwin C. Bliss, *Getting Things Done*, Bantam Books, 1976.
Peter F. Drucker, *The Effective Executive*, Pan Books, 1970.
Kathleen L. Hawkins & Peter Thurla, *Time Management Made Easy*, Panther Books, 1983.
Alan Lakein, *How to Get Control of Your Time and Your Life*, New America Library, 1973.
Alec R. MacKenzie, *The Time Trap*, McGraw-Hill, 1972.

Winston Marsh

Winston Marsh has won international renown for his inspiring and imaginative approaches to guarantee both companies and people incredible results for themselves and their customers. Every year he shares his secrets through his many keynote speaking assignments, books, articles and tapes to stimulate countless people to achieve the greatness that lies within them.

PART
3

HOW TO
Market
YOURSELF

by
Winston Marsh

All about you

> 'Happiness doesn't depend on the actual number of blessings we manage to scratch from life, only our attitude towards them.'
> — Alexander Solzhenitsyn

A new view of you

Let's take a new and different view of you.

Imagine that you are a can of beans on a supermarket shelf. You're just waiting for a potential customer to pick you off the shelf and buy you; to whisk you home so that you can begin the next stage of the game of life for beans.

If you were that can of beans how would you behave? What would your approach be when a customer walked past your shelf, stopped and looked you over?

You'd make certain that you stood proud and tall. You'd be sure that you had no dents; that your label was on straight; that you almost exuded the aroma of mouthwatering beans. In fact, you'd try to be the best looking can of beans on the shelf.

'Pick me, pick me,' your whole attitude would scream. All your efforts would be concentrated on providing the best view of yourself to make that person buy you. Not any other can. You.

When it's all said and done, people like you and I are really very much like a can of beans. Of course, we have the potential to do more, be more and achieve more than a can of beans but, still, we're like that can. Why? Because we too are products. Throughout our lives people will be looking us over on our shelf and deciding whether they will 'buy' us. Whether it is choosing us for a job or deciding whether they want us as a friend, they're making buying decisions about us.

They'll look very carefully at what we have to offer. How we present ourselves. Our special talents and skills. Our ability to deliver what we promise. People want to be sure we are the product that can answer their needs.

If we shape up, they'll buy. If not, no sale.

What people decide about you, the product, will be important throughout your life. Helping people to make a decision to choose you, whenever it's important, is what marketing yourself is all about.

You the product

It might help you to have a simple definition of 'product'. A product is merely a commodity, a promise to deliver, that can be offered for sale. Whether anybody buys the product is, of course, another matter.

So let's look at you. The product. What do you offer?

I couldn't possibly list all of the things that make you the unique person you are. But I bet I could list at least twenty without even knowing you well and with very little effort on my part.

Amazingly, most people really can't say very much about themselves when they're asked. Oh sure, they can probably talk about some of their failings. That seems to be easy. But talking about failings is crazy. Whoever bought a product on its bad points?

If you're going to be serious about marketing yourself you really must know yourself extremely well — the good, the bad and the ugly! You need to take the time to sit down and think about all the things that make you the person you are. And, after all, if you can't think of all these things then who can? You've lived with yourself longer than anybody else.

Find the time right now. Pick up your pen and make a list of all the things about yourself which you think would be important, and not so important, if we were trying to show the real you to the world. To help you get started, below is a list of thirty characteristics which can be found, in varying degrees, in people. Tick those that apply to you. Then think of as many others as you can which apply to you and add them to the list.

energetic	gracious	agreeable
understanding	confident	observant
soft-spoken	reserved	sincere
warm	cheerful	tactful
intelligent	witty	decisive
dominant	calm	serious
mature	enthusiastic	cooperative
bold	patient	thoughtful
frank	easy-going	modest
responsible	efficient	happy

See, already you're starting to know great things about yourself, the product.

The more we know about ourselves, the easier it becomes to market ourselves to others in any situation. If you can talk about your special talents and abilities in an easy, relaxed way, without sounding smart or boastful, others will see you as a positive and confident sort of person — the type of person who really is good to be around.

Selling or marketing

L et's talk about other people for a moment. There are two ways I could go about selling something.

The first way is the plain and simple, hard-sell method. All I do is find a product, get out there and knock on doors and ask people to buy it. If I ask enough people to buy, I'm bound to make sales.

For example, let's say my factory makes pens. Just the one simple sort of pen. A blue plastic retractable one that writes in black ink. To sell heaps of them, all I have to do is ask enough people whether they want a blue plastic retractable pen that writes in black ink. Even if I get lots of rejections, I'm bound to get some people who say yes, provided I ask enough people. To sell my entire stock is merely a matter of calling on sufficient people. I'll get a lot of knock-backs but I'll sell a lot of pens.

In this sort of selling we concentrate on telling people how great the product is and what it will do for them. If they like what we tell them, they'll buy. With the pen, for instance, I'd tell them how it can write under water or upside down and how the retractable refill means the ball point is protected and so on. The harder I sell, the better sales result. Putting it bluntly, this approach is really just flogging. You take a product and flog it to a customer, any customer, without paying any attention to what their real needs may be.

The second way is the marketing approach. First of all find out what my potential customer really needs. When I have identified those needs I carefully assess how my product fulfils those needs. If it does, making sales is simply a matter of showing the customers the solution to their needs. They will buy.

The marketing approach is all about identifying needs and answering them. In this fabulous book, 'How I Raised Myself From Failure To Success Through Selling', Frank Betger put it this way: 'Find out what a person needs, show them how to get it and they will move heaven and earth to get it.'

Harking back to the pen example, what if my approach was to get people talking about pens and what they do with them? I'd soon enough start to hear about their problems with pens and the things they really needed. Bingo! Once I hear a need, I can show

Find out how your customer thinks.

how my pen answers that need. Assuming it does, I've made a sale.

And there's another bonus with the marketing approach. You make far fewer calls for the same number of sales compared to the basic flogging approach. You see, once you have unearthed your market you can concentrate exclusively on that. You'll find out that there's a group of people with the same needs. Gradually it becomes easy for you to recognise people in that group. You concentrate on them rather than hitting the whole marketplace. Effectively, you've targetted your market for success.

So when it comes to selling my pens I don't ask anybody and everybody if they want a pen. Rather, I find out who the pen users are, get them talking about their needs, and then demonstrate how my pen answers those needs.

If you are to market yourself successfully in any sphere of your life — into a new job, a new social situation or a new relationship — you must first find out what the other person needs. Once you know that, you can then look at how you, the product, can provide the answer to those needs.

Decide on a target zone

In marketing anything to anyone, there are two parties to the sale: your customer and you. It is essential that both parties be relaxed, contented and happy after the sale is made.

In contrast to this, floggers tend not to stay around too long after the sale! They don't want to find out whether the customer is happy. So long as they are happy who cares? And they're ecstatic! They've got the sale, although they might not see too much repeat business.

If you're going to make sure that both parties are happy you'll need some guidelines. They are simple.

First of all, identify the needs of your potential customer. Then look at those needs from your own perspective and analyse how you personally feel about answering those needs. Ask yourself whether, in answering those needs, you will gain, benefit and grow as an individual. In other words, ask yourself whether you will see some of your own needs answered as a by-product of the sale.

Be tough!

Find out what people need and provide it.

Decide only to provide the solutions to your customers where, in doing so, you will also provide solutions for yourself. If you like where your customer's needs coincide with your own needs there is a zone of opportunity at which you should aim.

By focusing in on this zone of opportunity, you'll obviously be increasing the results and satisfaction you get from going about your business. As you help others solve their problems you'll solve yours in the process. You'll feel great!

It's not surprising that this result should occur. Zig Ziglar, one of America's most respected and quoted motivational speakers, puts it this way: 'You've got to give to get . . .

> **Help enough people get what they want and you'll get what you want.'**

The EC factors

Over the years I have worked with an incredible number of successful Australian business people. They have been the driving force behind the starting of new ventures, revitalising old ones and getting the best out of people and products. Each of these people have achieved incredible success that many of us could simply never even comprehend.

In working with each of them I have had the chance to get to know them and observe them closely, particularly in their early years of business building.

They are marketers to be ranked amongst the best. In identifying and answering the needs of others, they find the answers for their own aspirations. There are, however, two fundamental ingredients in their success. I call them the vital EC factors. So, what are those EC factors? Simple: enthusiasm and commitment.

Successful people are totally 100 per cent, absolutely enthusiastic about everything they and their people are planning, doing and dreaming. I only had to spend a few minutes with them while they literally bubbled about their ideas and projects before I too was infected with these people's passions. Their enthusiasm literally enveloped me and swept me along no matter how strong my doubts may have been initially.

I'm sure that this enthusiasm is the reason that people like this do so many things that others say simply can't be done.

And from where does the enthusiasm start? Quite simply, from their absolute commitment. Commitment to their projects and their plans, their dreams. Once they decide on a course of action they are totally and irrevocably committed to achieving it.

It is as if they lock their vision onto their goals so strongly and fiercely that they can almost savour the success of achievement before they take the first step.

Total, unwavering, single-minded commitment to the task at hand is surely the reason that they make so many things happen in such a short time.

The EC Factors — enthusiasm and commitment — are the key ingredients in successfully marketing yourself and your talents to anybody.

In my role as a speaker and advisor I meet lots of people in business, some doing well, really well, and others not going too well at all. I tend to rate them on their EC factors. Almost, without exception, the result is the same.

People with education and talent but no enthusiasm and commitment are always being out-rated, out-performed and out-marketed by people with no education and talent but loads of enthusiasm and commitment.

This, in my belief, is the key to successfully marketing yourself and your abilities to others. Enthusiasm and commitment are all-powerful.

Being positive

When it's all boiled down, the enthusiasm and commitment factors come down to just one thing: your attitude. How positive are you? How do you feel about yourself, what you're doing now and where you're going in the future?

Positive people produce spectacular results.

Because they are enthusiastic about what they're doing and committed to achieving their goals they can smell the scent of victory, can taste the fruit of success, well before they reach them.

It's a fact that people like to buy from people who are positive; people whose enthusiasm literally sweeps others along and makes them feel good too; people whose commitment keeps them at it long after lesser people have quit.

Now, let's see whether you're ready to market yourself. Check out how positive your attitude is and whether you've got those fires of enthusiasm and commitment burning in your belly.

Rate yourself on this check list by circling the figure which corresponds with how you feel about each statement. Be frank, be honest, be realistic.

	All of the time	Most of the time	Some of the time	Very occa- sionally	Never
1. I feel good about myself.	5	4	3	2	1
2. I really love my work.	5	4	3	2	1
3. I enjoy whatever I'm doing.	5	4	3	2	1
4. I love getting up in the morning.	5	4	3	2	1
5. Every day is really a great day.	5	4	3	2	1
6. I can't wait to get back to what I'm doing.	5	4	3	2	1
7. I know and build on my strong points.	5	4	3	2	1
8. I'm working to improve my shortcomings.	5	4	3	2	1
9. I have clearly defined goals in both my business and my personal life.	5	4	3	2	1
10. Other people seem to like to be around me.	5	4	3	2	1
11. I'm at ease talking to other people.	5	4	3	2	1
12. I like getting other people involved.	5	4	3	2	1
13. I finish what I start.	5	4	3	2	1
14. This year will be even more successful for me than last year.	5	4	3	2	1
15. I reckon I'm enthusiastic.	5	4	3	2	1

	All of the time	Most of the time	Some of the time	Very occa-sionally	Never
16. Problems are really fun to solve.	5	4	3	2	1
17. People say I'm cheerful and positive.	5	4	3	2	1
18. I really do like people.	5	4	3	2	1
19. Difficult people don't affect my outlook.	5	4	3	2	1
20. I control my situation.	5	4	3	2	1
Total score					

If you scored 80 or above, you rate really well on the EC factor scale. You are positive about yourself and your future. You are ready or are about to market yourself to success.

If you scored between 50 and 80, you've probably got a few reservations about yourself and where you're going. You should reflect on all of the great assets you have and remind yourself of the importance of what you want to achieve in life. Come on, you can get excited about your life!

A rating below 50 means that you must go back to the basics and decide what is important to you and why. Then get some clear goals that turn you on and organise yourself to reach them. You should carefully read Daniel's and Lisa's section of this book again.

Looking good, feeling good

There's a saying that beauty is more than skin deep and nothing could be more true when it comes to marketing yourself. If victory, success or achievement came only to good looking people, then how come movie stars don't run the country? Good looks don't equate to success anymore than good education or great talent will produce success. It's the total person that counts. When it comes to how we look, remember:

It isn't how you look, it's what you do with what you've got!

• When you feel good about yourself, you produce great results. So what do these two statements mean? Simply, that we must make sure we do the very best with our physical appearance and then wear a mental attitude to match.

It's worth taking time and trouble to find out the fashions, colours and styles that suit and complement our physical looks. Certainly, my self-image really changed when I took the time to visit a colour consultant. She told me colours to wear that I never dreamed I could. Now when I wear them I really do feel fantastic. Look good, and feel great. Make a point of finding out the name of someone who can help you dress for success.

And take special care about your physical appearance too. Keep your hair well groomed, clothes neat and tidy and so on. Maybe too, if you're a few kilograms over your correct weight, you should aim to get rid of the excess flab. When you do, you'll feel so much better about yourself physically that your mental attitude will leap ahead. There'll be literally nothing you can't tackle and win.

You never get a second chance at creating a good first impression.

It's worthwhile filling out the check list below as a way of finding out whether you're doing the best you can with the way you look. Rate yourself on each area, honestly and objectively.

If you rate above 40 then you probably feel as good as you look. Between 25 and 40 means that just a little effort is necessary to get yourself up to scratch.

Under 25 means that you really must get serious about how you look. Right now you should set yourself some goals about your appearance and then concentrate on reaching them.

	Always	Most of the time	Rarely
1. I'm about the right weight for my height.	5	3	1
2. I look vital and alive.	5	3	1
3. I am committed to regular exercise.	5	3	1
4. My hair is right for style, length and general grooming.	5	3	1
5. My fingernails are manicured and my hands clean.	5	3	1
6. My teeth are polished and well looked after.	5	3	1
7. My dress is appropriate for me and each particular situation.	5	3	1
8. The jewellery I wear is suitable for the occasion.	5	3	1
9. I look neat and tidy (uncrumpled, clean shoes and tidy).	5	3	1
10. Overall, I think my image is really good.	5	3	1
Total score			

Opportunity is everywhere

One more thing. Marketing is very much a frame of mind. When you've made up your mind to become a marketer, and you develop your marketing consciousness, you're bound to see opportunities everywhere. These opportunities are really needs crying out to be answered. Provided you have the skills, talent and abilities to satisfy those needs, then you've got yourself some new customers. You'll find that the mere fact that you understand a few marketing principles stimulates an often long-dormant ability in you to recognise and grab opportunity.

Getting it all together

> **'The intellectual's problem is not vision, it's commitment.' — Trevor Griffiths**

It's planned attitude that counts

Of course, having the right attitude to marketing is largely determined by whether you have a plan for marketing yourself. Like most things, it is much easier to be confident about something if you know where you are going.

> ## If you don't know where you are going, any road will get you there.

The best way to market anything, and certainly yourself, is to have a plan — a simple idea of where you are going and how you're going to get there.

Unfortunately, many people are not renowned for the enthusiasm with which they set down their plans, for either their business or their personal lives. In fact, business or marketing plans are notorious for their absence rather than for their presence.

And the absence of these plans really shows.

The staggering statistic is that 8 out of 10 business people have never put their plans down on paper. Very few have a simple plan that tells them where they are heading. It means that when most people get out of bed each day, they wait for something to happen just because they've got nothing really planned. They get carried along like flotsam and jetsam in the sea of life.

The bottom-line result is that 80 per cent of all businesses operating today will be out of business within 10 years. Most people plan to fail by failing to plan.

Eight out of ten businesses fail.

And as far as individuals go, most people will never achieve their ambition or potential because they never set down a plan to do so.

SWOT for success

One of the best ways in which the facts can be gathered to produce your marketing plan, is by doing a personal SWOT (strengths, weaknesses, opportunities and threats) analysis. In undertaking a SWOT analysis of yourself, you look at your strengths and weaknesses and the oportunities and threats which face you. Then you set goals to achieve your most important objectives.

There is a great side benefit in doing this because it becomes a highly motivational experience as you plan to achieve your potential. You start to feel that you can achieve your aims because, like most people, you'll find that setting your goals is the hardest part. I believe that setting your goals is at least 60 per cent of the effort required to achieve them. In other words, you're over halfway there just because you thought them through.

When you do your SWOT, set aside ample time without distraction. About half a day is ideal.

THE S.W.O.T. ANALYSIS

STRENGTHS. WEAKNESSES. OPPORTUNITIES THREATS.

A SWOT session is not a time for personal criticism. Rather it is a free-ranging assessment of your overall position. Therefore, every thought is important. Whenever you think of a strength, for instance, it should be recorded. Under no circumstances should you make a value judgment on that strength or try to justify it. Similarly, too, items that you see as strengths may also be perceived as weaknesses. If so, don't worry, record them under both headings. The rule which should apply to the whole exercise is:

'If it's worth thinking, it's worth writing down.'

First, list all of your strengths. This should take you 15 to 30 minutes. Most people will find at least 20 to 30 strengths.

Then spend the same time thinking about your weaknesses and list them. You will find about the same number of weaknesses as stengths.

Next, think about the threats to your future and the opportunities for yourself that you could capitalise on. You will probably find between 10 and 15 opportunities and threats in the 15 to 20 minutes you should devote to each of these categories.

Once you have the findings of your SWOT analysis you can move to the next stage. Consider all of the evidence about yourself that the analysis has revealed and then answer the following question: 'What are the most important five things in your life right now that you must do in the light of the strengths, weaknesses, opportunities and threats that you have identified.

The strategy behind asking for the most important five things is simple. Time-management techniques indicate that we, as individuals, can handle only five extra tasks effectively. If we therefore choose only five tasks then we really have a chance of achieving them.

Once you've decided on your five objectives, give each of them a target date by which you will aim to have them completed. Think through the strategies you'll need to adopt to achieve each of them. Break them down into small easily reached steps, if necessary.

Write down both your objectives and your strategies to achieve them and put them somewhere you can readily refer to them. In thinking them through make sure you consider the answers to these three questions in respect of each objective:

Where am I now?

Where do I want to be?

How am I going to get there?

Now you've got a plan. You've got the things you really see as important — the things to work on that really concern you.

Be realistic

O ne word of warning as you go about writing your marketing plan. Remember that sometimes you can get caught
up by the magic and motivation of goal-setting and there is
a tendency to set unrealistic goals. It's best, in preparing your
first marketing plan, to aim your sights just a little lower than you
might otherwise wish. Often the first fresh flush of enthusiasm for
marketing yourself is replaced by disillusionment as time elapses

and obstacles are met. It is best, therefore, to suspect that the results you achieve in the first year will not be those that you are ultimately capable of later on. Nonetheless they will be far better than what you'd do with no plan at all. Be careful, of course, that you don't become too pessimistic, otherwise you may produce a self-fulfilling prophecy.

The magic mix of marketing

When you are preparing your marketing plan you need to give some thought to the critical four elements that make up what is known as the 'marketing mix'. Just as the key to successfully baking a cake is the right blend or mix of ingredients, so too is the correct mix of vital ingredients the key to devising a successful marketing plan.

There are only four ingredients in the mix of your marketing cake. Without proper consideration of each there is no way that you will prepare a marketing plan that will produce the success you seek.

The ingredients are:

- product — what you really offer a purchaser;
- price — the apparent cost of what you offer;
- distribution (or place) — how or where people buy your product; and
- promotion — how people get to hear about your product.

Before I continue, let me remind you that I'm primarily talking about the best way of marketing you, the individual, to potential employers, colleagues and friends. I'm not talking so much about how you might tackle selling other products or your specific business activity although, with just a little bit of thought, you'll be able to adapt these principles to any situation.

Product

I've talked a little about you as a product in an earlier section of this book. What I asked you to do then was to get to know all about yourself, and to know the things that make you the unique person you are. Now we need to take that process another step. We need to portray you, the product, so that other people can recognise what you offer and, more particularly, what you will do for them — how you will answer their needs.

And you really have to tell people what you can do very simply. So simply, that they will have no trouble understanding what you offer and how good it will be for them. Let me give you an example.

Occasionally, I meet disillusioned life assurance sales people who are fairly new to their business. They're upset because every time they go to a party someone asks what they do. When they answer, 'I sell life assurance,' suddenly they're alone.

Why does it happen? Simple. Everybody thinks that life assurance sales people are second cousins to Ned Kelly and are scared they might get sold something. That's why they disappear. Later on, when they know what life assurance can do, they change their opinion but, at first they are very wary. (There's an old saying that people hate life assurance but they love what it can do.)

So what advice do I give these life assurance people who are worried that they've got the plague or a malfunctioning deodorant?

The answer is easy. I tell them to get their product right. You see, they're not in the life assurance business, they're in the money business. Life assurance is simply the means that is used to protect, guarantee, invest and deliver money for people whenever it's needed.

Next time they are asked what they do, they simply and disarmingly answer, 'I'm in the money business.'

What is one of the great people motivators? Money! Most people like talking about it, chasing it, accumulating it and spending it. Once they hear that reply, the average person relaxes and responds along the lines of, 'Great! I've got a few dollars that I was thinking of . . .'

My point is that when you get the product right and express it in a way that the prospect understands, they'll want to talk about it.

At first thought, when it comes to marketing themselves, most people would probably think that there is very little difference between what they have to offer and what anyone else has to offer. But that is just not the case.

Put yourself in the buyer's shoes.

Can they clearly see what you have to offer them in terms that are easily understood, simple and appealing? Is the product exciting, different and chock full of benefits for them?

Think about the purchases that you make. Do you always look for products that are exactly the same as everything else? Or would you rather seek out a product that is exciting, appears different and seems to best answer your particular needs? A product that literally taps you on the shoulder and says, 'Buy me, because . . .' When you find one that does, very often other considerations, such as price, are not important. Once you find something that clearly says what it is and how it answers your needs you are irresistibly drawn to it, like a bee to a honey pot.

The real problem is that we tend to look after ourselves and our capabilities through our own eyes rather than through the eyes of the prospective purchasers of our services. We see our talents without the tinsel, our abilities expressed in cold, hard, clinical, unemotional terms. There's no razzmatazz, no 'pick me, pick me' pointers for the prospective purchaser.

Mentally step back and take a look at yourself, your skills and abilities. Look at what you do best, what you would like to do better and what you enjoy doing most. Then look at the other things that you do only because you think you have to. Chances are that what you do well and what you enjoy doing probably account for the majority of your activity, income and satisfaction.

On the other hand, when you assess what you dislike doing you will find that you derive far less income and satisfaction for the time you spend doing them. On a time-expended comparison with the revenue and satisfaction you get, they are probably not worthwhile.

So it makes sense to promote the things you enjoy doing when you talk to people to whom you are marketing yourself. Leave the things you don't like doing for other people who probably enjoy doing them.

It makes sense to promote the things you enjoy doing.

You'll have the best chance of success in marketing those things that you do well and enjoy doing provided of course that other people have a need for them.

No mattter what you decide, once you've got your product defined start to tell people about it in clear and simple terms. Make sure you stress the benefits to them.

Above all, be enthusiastic about yourself because you are the product.

Know what benefits the client will receive by using you.

For example, you may believe that you have great sales skills. After establishing that your potential purchaser needs someone

with those skills, explain that you have the ability to achieve their goals for them in the sales arena. Clearly and confidently tell them why you can perform. And, of course, stress the real benefit to them: making more money!

It may all sound a little emotional. If it does, fine! I have yet to meet the person who doesn't get emotional about their business, particularly about making money.

Price

Nobody expects to get anything, or a person of quality like you, for nothing. What they do like to do is get it, or you, as cheaply as possible! Therefore, what you need to do is to make sure that people pay an amount which is fair and realistic for what you offer.

> **People only make judgments based on price in the absence of anything else on which to compare.**

In fact, people tend to believe that the more they pay, the better the product. Two examples are worth thinking about.

Imagine you have a heart attack and collapse on the footpath. Two men rush up and, through your pain, they tell you they are doctors. Would you ask each for a quote? Of course not. You want what they offer whatever it might cost. Strange enough, if they did quote, you'd probably take the higher price because most people believe that the more they pay for a product or service the better it must be!

Imagine that you want some work done around your house. Because what you are likely to spend is substantial you obtain three quotes. One comes in very low, one is in the middle and one is high. If price were the only determinant you would take the low one, wouldn't you? Wrong. Consumer behaviour tells us that most likely you'll choose between either the middle or the higher price. You'll eliminate the lower price automatically. This could be because both quotes promise what appears to be better service or better delivery or better completion dates or whatever. Even if they don't, you probably just expect that there will be something wrong with the lowest quote. Yet we tend to forget this personal experience when we think about prices for our services.

The true price for your services, your talents, skills and abilities is whatever the market can stand. The market will pay whatever it is charged provided it believes it gets value. Two people can therefore provide seemingly identical products but have quite different prices. In a nutshell, if what you deliver generates a high degree of satisfaction and confirms the feeling that you deliver a first class product then your price will be met.

Finally, remember the price equation:

Price = dollar cost + service.

If you provide no service, people can only compare the dollar cost. The greater you make the service element, the higher the price can be. When it comes to marketing yourself, the service element is made up of factors such as delivering what you promised, when you promised it and how you promised it. It's making sure that you get feedback and that you keep monitoring and building your clients' satisfaction. Above all it's making sure that you maintain the EC factor, that your enthusiasm is infectious and your commitment to your clients' objectives is total.

Distribution (or place)

This ingredient is perhaps a little hard to understand when you are the product. What it really means is how or where people get what you have to offer.

To make it simpler, let's look at an example in the retail business world.

Up until quite recently, the usual way people (at least in the metropolitan areas) went shopping was to drive to a shopping centre. It could be either the traditional strip shopping centre or, more frequently, the newer shopping complexes containing one or more vast department stores surrounded by a ring of smaller, specialist stores. People went there and bought.

Now this is all changing. The change has come about as a result of catalogues and credit cards. How? Quite simple.

Now people really can shop from home. They don't need to travel to the shopping centre. They receive a great big catalogue in their letter box full of colour photographs of just about everything for sale in the store. They literally read through the catalogue (or rather look at the pictures) and simply make their decision.

They then phone the store and order what they want. They don't even have to mail a cheque or drive over and pay. They merely quote their credit card number and the store does the rest. It picks the items off the shelves, packs them and delivers them. All without the customer leaving home.

So there you are. A new way of distributing retail products to consumers. The old and the new. Both work, but perhaps one is fading into the past and one looks like the future.

So, how then do you distribute what you have to offer? When it comes to your personal talents and abilities, it has to be in person. You really do have to front up and deliver the goods, at least in your business role.

On a personal basis, however, there are lots of ways you can distribute yourself to your market. For example, it's that visit to a friend to congratulate them on an achievement or to commiserate with them on a defeat.

Perhaps, it's that unexpected letter you write, giving of yourself, to someone who needs to hear from you. Maybe it's simply a phone call to someone to say, 'I love you,' or more simply to ask, 'How are things?'

Distribution. It's the simple secret of how you share yourself around to the people whose needs you can answer.

Promotion

This element of the mix is what most people really think is marketing. People believe that marketing is all about advertising, promotion and generally beating a big bass drum to excite potential customers to buy.

Nothing could be further from the truth. In fact, if you get the product, price and distribution right then you really do need very little promotion to market your product.

Remember, if you answer people's needs, they will move heaven and earth to get those answers.

Unfortunately, people won't know what you have to offer unless they hear about it. That's where promotion comes in. You need to tell people what you've got. Otherwise it's a bit like a man winking at a woman in the dark. He might know his intentions but nothing is achieved until she knows them. You've got to be noticed.

Promotion is all about getting noticed. Even more than that, it's about being noticed by the right people, your potential market. Promoting to the wrong people is a waste of time, effort and money. In the previous example, it would be just like the man's wink getting through to the guy sitting next to the lady. The message gets through but to the wrong, totally wrong, consumer and probably with disastrous results!

To be effective then, your promotional effort must be relevant to, and targetted at, your desired market. Then it must be delivered by the most efficient and economical method. And that method is probably not advertising. Unless you're very good at writing adverts, you'll probably waste your money.

Far better to get your message across in more effective, more personal ways. The best way you can tell people what you've got is on a face-to-face basis, when they can not only hear the product but also see it.

So take some time to think. Have a long philosophical look at what you've got and what you want. Work on who would want what you've got to offer and make a list of those people. Then go and see them, one by one.

It takes guts and determination to get out there and meet with your market but it's worth it.

For example, a staggering fact is that 40 per cent of all job vacancies are never advertised. They are filled by someone who gets off their backside and talks to a person with a need for somebody like them.

Two other ways can work wonders for you too.

Firstly, a well-composed letter or phone call can be an excellent way of getting to your target market. The letter or phone call needs to highlight the solution to your prospect's need up front (which gets their attention and gets them to want to find out more). Once they're reading or listening you can show them how you provide those answers (or, better still, excite them enough that they'll want to meet you in person).

The best approach is the combination of a letter followed up by a phone call two or three days later.

If you follow up a letter you will find that it really does work.

Secondly, getting a referral from a third party is an extremely successful way of promoting yourself. If somebody is happy with what you've done for them, they are happy to tell others. To capitalise on this, all you need do is make sure you find out the names of the other people they've told about you. Generally, they'll be happy to tell you their names and, if you do it right, you can probably get a few more recommendations.

Once you find out who knows about you, all you need to do is contact them. Chances are that you'll be welcomed because they'll see you as having answers to their problems or needs.

Marketing yourself is easy!

Making it happen

'Think before you think!' — Stanislaw Lec

Now that you've got your marketing tactics all together, your next step is critical. You've got to get out there and meet your potential customers. It's easy. Here's how you go about making the sale.

Decide your target market

Successfully selling yourself has its basis in deciding which combination of your talents and abilities you want to sell and to whom.

Selling is not a shotgun affair.

You do not just load a shotgun with pellets about yourself and fire it hopefully into the air with the general idea that one of your good points might strike somebody and score.

Rather, you decide what you want to market and then look at the characteristics of the people in the marketplace who could possibly be buyers of that product.

Do you need a reminder on how you decide what to market? You review all of the things that you do and especially look for those that you do particularly well. Then narrow the list down by deciding which of those things you really enjoy doing. Now you've determined what you have to market.

Develop a profile or a thumbnail sketch of your potential customers. Review them carefully. See if there is some common thread running through the people you would like to do business with. If there is, this probably suggests that you have a special ability or understanding with 'birds of a feather' — a useful advantage.

Once you have got a real or imagined profile of your potential clients it is much easier to produce a short list of names that fit that profile. You can assemble this from people you know, local papers, mailing lists, the yellow pages and directories by simply matching names against your customer profile.

Now you've got a list of 'suspects'. What we have got to do is turn those suspects into prospects.

Do your homework

Now is the time to find out as much as you possibly can about the people or companies on your suspect list. Try and get an annual report, their price lists, brochures, and so on. Talk to other people in their industry, their suppliers and customers to learn more. Talk to their friends, neighbours and competitors and discover as much as you possibly can about them.

Do your homework.

The more homework you do the more likely you are to be successful. You are not looking for inane generalities but rather something that may suggest that there is a possibility that they need your talents.

Gradually, you will form a picture about them and decide whether they have a need for you. Even if there doesn't seem to be a need at first glance don't strike them off your list. Perhaps, when you get to talk to them, you may find the need is there. It may just be well disguised.

Once your homework has been done and you have unearthed a need for your services, you can move on to the next step.

Show them a 'what's in it for me'

T o turn a suspect into a prospect you need to 'qualify' them. Suspects become prospects when you confirm that:

- there is a need for your service;
- they can afford to pay for it; and
- they are prepared to buy if convinced.

When the answer to each of these questions is 'yes', you have what sales people call a 'red hot' prospect.

You can't determine the answer to those questions from a distance or without talking to your suspect on their home ground. There is simply no other way. No matter how much you dislike it, you really have to get to the suspect and talk to them to qualify them.

Getting your appointment with the decision maker is critical. It's no use dealing with people who will only pass the buck. Your homework will have told you the key person to whom you must talk.

There are two ways you can do this. You can pick up that magic device — the telephone — and ring and ask for an appointment. This is generally the easiest and most effective way if you are not frightened of cold canvassing on the phone.

Alternatively, you can write a letter to your targeted decision maker. It's a fact that letters won't produce the same results that phone calls do. Nevertheless, letters do work and will produce acceptable results provided you follow them up.

The objective of the telephone call or the letter is not to sell your services. Rather, it is to gain you an appointment so that you have the opportunity to sell on a face-to-face basis.

The phone call or letter must therefore contain a 'what's in it for me' for your suspect that will motivate them to want to find out more. A 'what's in it for me' is a clearly expressed, simply understood benefit statement designed to grab your suspect's attention. It should excite them and make them want to know more.

Put yourself in your suspect's shoes.

Think about their likely problems and try and come up with a compelling statement that attracts their attention and excites their interest. But that's all. Remember it's only to attract attention and excite interest. Don't try and tell them, or sell them, either on the telephone or in your letter. Keep that for your meeting. Your approach must be the same as Lady Godiva's. Reveal enough to excite interest, conceal enough to demand further examination.

Do it well and you've got the appointment. Make sure that it's always at their office.

Learn to 'chat people up' professionally

Allow yourself plenty of time when you go for the appointment. Try and get to your suspect's office about ten minutes before your appointment. This will give you time to have a chat to the receptionist, your target's secretary or any-body else you can find.

If you've got your ears, eyes and other senses tuned it's amazing what you can learn in a few minutes from the people who know most about the company — the staff.

By using the famous 'How's things?' question, and asking staff members, 'What's happening?' you will gain knowledge and infor-mation that may assist in your interview. Carefully note all of the information you glean and file it in your memory bank. It may be handy when you are sitting across the desk from your suspect.

Know the 'W' questions to get them talking

Once you are in front of your suspect it's time to move into the selling mode. This is where most people fail. They believe the selling mode is to instantly grab the suspect's attention and immediately launch into an exposition of their capabilities and attributes. They figure the suspect will be so bowled over they will just want to buy as soon as possible. Not so, regrettably. The suspect doesn't want to be assailed by facts, figures and flights of fancy. Not initially, anyway.

The first step in the face-to-face contact is to establish communication. And communication means listening rather than talking.

The great architect in his wisdom gave each of us two eyes, two ears and only one mouth. This would suggest that eyes and ears should be used about four times as much as the mouth. Roughly then, every interview you have of a selling nature should be 80 per cent listening and 20 per cent talking.

Your first act must be to get your suspect talking about themselves and their company.

Your sole objective should be to listen, listen, listen.

Listen carefully to what the suspect is saying and particularly listen for clues to what their needs may be.

Get them to talk about the subject that a great advertisement so succinctly summarises as 'the most important thing in the world' — themselves.

To do this it's only necessary to know the 'W' questions. Ask them who, where, which, when, what, why and how. Ask them about themselves and about their business. Get them talking and you will see your suspect relax and become much more amenable as they talk to you about themselves, their triumphs and their tribulations.

Listen and hear the needs

When your suspect talks, listen to what they are telling you. If you sustain the converation with the 'W' questions you must hear your suspect's needs, desires and demands.

When conversation lags, just ask another 'W' question to get it going again. While the suspect talks, start qualifying them as a prospect by listening to the clues that will answer those questions. Is there a need for you? Can they afford you? Are they prepared to buy if convinced? Whether they qualify as prospects will become very apparent to you as you listen, listen, listen.

When it's your turn, fill a need

Once you have done your share of listening, target the major need you have unearthed for which you believe you have the answer. When it is your turn to talk, explain simply and directly the way that you can fill that need. Keep your explanation simple and concentrate on explaining how the solution will benefit them.

Don't be tricked by your own familiarity with your capabilities and go into intimate, boring detail. Just concentrate on showing your prospect that you have the answer to their needs.

Your sole objective is to show them very simply and succinctly how you will provide a real benefit, a compelling 'what's in it for me' for them.

When you're selling intangibles, like yourself and your abilities, you need to recognise that there is an extra step needed to ensure success. If you are selling tangibles, like motor cars or baked beans, the product itself reinforces the benefits because the prospect can touch, taste or test it.

In selling yourself the extra step is:

Find a way to make tangible the intangible.

For example, what you are offering is maybe a special skill that could reduce the time required for the prospect to complete a project. Don't merely say that you will save them time. Tell them this means more time with their family, or on the beach, or a weekend they don't have to work.

The more you make the intangibles tangible, the more you'll see the prospect nod in agreement. From there it's just a short step to the nod of approval.

Keep control of the follow-up

Never leave an interview on the basis that your prospect will call you. No matter how enthused they might be, their enthusiasm will decrease rapidly as time elapses. The longer it is since you highlighted their need and gave them the answer to it, the less inclined they will be to follow through. It's a natural reaction. More urgent tasks, pressure of work, the boss's demands and so on, will all combine to prevent them picking up the phone to follow through or focus on making a decision.

Factors like 'buyer's remorse', which attacks after a person has made a decision to buy, can also come into it. This means that they have second thoughts about a course of action and this happens simply because you are not there to keep reminding them of the benefits.

No matter how enthused your prospect becomes when you're with them you can't afford to lose control of the follow-up process. Before you conclude your appointment make sure you agree on a course of action with your prospect which leaves you firmly in the driver's seat. You must be the one who makes the phone calls. You must be the one that initiates the action. If you're in this position you can bring the whole exercise to a successful conclusion.

Keep it simple

The 'KISS' principle — keep it simple stupid — applies here. Keep your discussions in simple terms. Don't use industry jargon or big words. Use simple language that everyone can understand.

Complicated language and jargon is called 'fog' and many people are very talented at generating fog. They like to prove how professional and competent they are in terms that the layperson doesn't understand. Understand that if prospects are familiar with most of the terms you use they probably don't need you.

Most of us aren't interested in knowing what the motor of a car looks like when we go to buy a car. All we want to know is how smooth the ride is. So it is with the sale of ourselves. Prospects aren't really looking to know our life story, but rather what we will do for them.

Cut down the fog.

Of course, on occasions prospects will want to know something about your professional background or experience. In that case, give them an uncomplicated answer, but don't read them the book.

The same applies to any written presentation or resumé. If you want to leave one or are asked to provide one make sure that it doesn't go on and on. One or two pages for most is ample. The rest of those multi-paged productions is often puffery and is generally just an excuse to cover inadequacies.

Follow up and follow through

Having agreed on a course of action after the interview you need to stick to it. If you have promised to send further information for instance, make sure that becomes a priority and that your prospect gets it within a few days. Perhaps you could even deliver it personally. There are huge advantages in personally dropping off information. It enables you to accelerate the follow-up process.

And then comes the follow through. Make sure that you ring to confirm that the details were received and that your prospect understands them. Then ring, or preferably visit, as arranged to get their decision. Your prospect may want to procrastinate — it's human — and defer making a decision as long as possible. With you in control this need not be a worry. Regular phone contact will soon have a decision made one way or the other. With an approach like this the decision will usually be in your favour.

Once a decision has been made to buy, you must do something quickly to make tangible the fact that the sale has been made. Drop them a note or find another gesture that gets the agreement between you confirmed.

So that's it

Simple, isn't it? Selling yourself is just like selling anything, except that the product is very special; it's you! You are worth an investment of all the time and energy possible to ensure that your talents and abilities provide enjoyable and worthwhile solutions for both your purchaser and yourself. Go to it!

Action Steps

To help you to act immediately on what you have just read, we have listed **Ten guaranteed steps to success** for each part of this book. Act now!

Part 1   *How to Motivate Yourself*

1. Give yourself a daily dose of motivation
2. Be aware of your motive for every action you undertake
3. Know the purpose of your life so that your framework of goals is built on a rock-solid foundation.
4. Ensure you have some written goals in each major area of your life: emotional, mental, spiritual, physical, social financial.
5. Read regularly about successful people you admire for inspiration and encouragement in your own life.
6. Have a written 'What's in it for me?' list to support each of your goals with burning desire.
7. Ensure that you begin achieving your goal immediately by using the French breadstick method.
8. Take control of your environment. Make it help rather than hinder you. Surround yourself with positive people and positive information whenever possible.
9. Always be a part of the solution and not part of the problem.
10. Dwell on positive thoughts, ideas and scripture and tune out the negative inner voice. Have faith! Get the facts! And the feelings will follow.

Part 2   *How to Manage Yourself*

When it comes to managing yourself we focused on building your energy levels, planning and personal organization. Here are ten action steps that you can implement immediately:

1. Begin a regular program of exercise.

2. Create, repeat and believe in your own series of positive affirmations.

3. Wake up five minutes earlier tomorrow morning.

4. Invest a maximum of three hours creating a yearly planner.

5. Write your short, specific, measurable 'to do list' this afternoon/evening for tomorrow.

6. Focus your mind and energy on the highest priority task at hand.

7. Sort out your physical environment and eliminate all clutter.

8. Create a master list of all uncompleted projects in your life.

9. Combine all your personal reference books (i.e. diary & address books, etc.) into a time management diary system.

10. With all lists you create establish priorities based on the importance of the activity, not the sequence of when you wish to complete them.

Part 3   How to Market Yourself

1. Take a new view of you.

2. Find out your potential customer needs.

3. Target your market.

4. Help people get what they want.

5. Be enthusiastic and committed.

6. Be positive to produce spectacular results.

7. Make sure you look good so as to feel great.

8. Write yourself a plan.

9. Get the marketing mix right.

10. Get out there and tell people to sell people.

It is time to stop reading and start doing. Before you put this book down make a commitment to yourself. Decide what action you will take immediately in order to enjoy the biggest benefit to your life.

Author's note

We, the authors of this book, would love to hear from you. We appreciate your feedback, your comments and your stories about personal growth and development. Maybe we can use your story and experience in our next book.

Please write to any one of us at our addresses below. We will circulate your letter to the others on request.

Lisa McInnes-Smith
Cassette Learning Systems Pty Ltd
7 Panorama Court
Bulleen Vic. 3105
Tel: (03) 850 1492
Fax: (03) 852 0498

Daniel Johnson
Daniel Johnson Presentations
254 North Road
Brighton East 3187
Tel: (03) 530 6200
Fax: (03) 530 6211

Winston Marsh
Winston Marsh Pty Ltd
10 Johnson Street
Oakleigh Vic 3169
Tel: (03) 569 1100
Fax: (03) 569 1181

For further copies of this book please contact any one of us.

For information regarding speaking engagements, and other books and programs by these authors, contact the authors individually.

Wishing you a happy forever!

NOTES

NOTES

NOTES